I0172500

Loop, Knot, Repeat

Running Through Life, Motherhood, and Mumbai

Nandini Sampat

/ BookLeaf
Publishing

India | USA | UK

Dedication

For my family,
who steady my stride and share my journey,
and to Mumbai,
the city that carries me.

Preface

This book began with a single step.

Running has always been more than a sport for me. It is discipline, freedom, ritual and rebellion. It is where I meet my body, wrestle with my mind, and make peace with both. Each run begins with the same act: loop, knot, repeat. The tying of laces, the start of a journey. That rhythm has shaped not just my running, but my life.

I have run my city, Mumbai, in the quiet before dawn, through its monsoon rains, beneath its unforgiving sun. These streets, sometimes broken, sometimes gleaming, have carried me, tested me, and taught me resilience. Running here is never just about the distance; it is about belonging to a place that is chaotic, crowded, alive, and endlessly forgiving. It is a love letter to the city I grew up in, the people of this city who, knowingly or unknowingly, run beside me in spirit, and to the country that has shaped me.

Running is personal, but it is never solitary. It takes a village, it creates community, and it leaves us altered. This collection is my attempt to honour that through rhythm, breath, and the pulse of language that mirrors the run itself. I have had many companions on the road, shoes worn thin, music that carried me, the strength of my family who share in the sacrifices and triumphs, the friends and strangers who cheer along the way, the people who inspire and train me, and with every kilometre words began to take shape. These poems are fragments of those experiences.

It is also the journey of a mother. Running has taught me patience when I had none, courage when doubt weighed heavy, and endurance when exhaustion took over. Some days I ran to escape, some days to find myself. It has shown me how to stumble, rise, and keep moving.

The poems move from the individual to the collective, from solitude to strength and finally to legacy, closing with the hope that my children too might find their own stride in this world. I offer them to you, not as answers, but as markers along the path. May you find echoes of your own story here.

This is not a manual on running. It is a tribute: to the road, to the body, to persistence and to possibilty.

It is about running, but it is also about life.

Acknowledgements

This book, like every run, is never mine alone.

I owe the deepest gratitude to my family. To my husband, Mihir, and my children, Arjun and Varun, for the patience, love, and strength they gave me through every early morning, late night, and long absence. You steadied me when I faltered and reminded me why I run in the first place.

To my parents, Anand and Brinda Somaya, for instilling in me both discipline and imagination, and to my brother, Vikram, for always running beside me in spirit. To my aunt Viju, whose presence through every endeavour has been a constant source of strength, support and joy in my life.

To my childhood friends and running buddies, whose cheers, conversations, and quiet encouragement have carried me further than I could have gone alone.

To my running coach, Nakul Butta of All In Running: you continue to teach, inspire, and challenge me. I am forever grateful. You gave me the supreme gift of completing my first marathon, of surviving and thriving in the complex and intricate world of running, and most of all, of keeping me on the road day after day. The AIR community brings together an incredible group of runners from whom I continuously learn and draw inspiration.

To Sohrab Khushrushahi, Sneha Shah and the team at SOHFIT: you made me strong, put me on the path of fitness, and gave me my first insight into the world of running.

To the streets of Mumbai, which gave me not just a path to run but a place to belong.

And finally, to you who read this: the distance doesn't matter, the pace doesn't matter, and not every run will give you peace. What matters is that you just start to run. The rest—the struggle, the rhythm, the release—will find you on the road.

1. Before the City Wakes

It is quiet.
It is dark.
Just the streetlight.

The road is like a mirror,
glistening in the dark.
The rain comes and goes,
washing over me.
I hop on the raised concrete,
But the craters
are too deep.

Wet feet,
means crimped toes,
means battered toe nails.
But I forge onward,
into the darkness,

To the familiar sight
of the man
pushing his cycle
up the flyover.
To the bright lights
of the petrol station,

1

that stands like a beacon
in the darkness.

As a woman,
you know where each light falls,
where each figure sits,
where each security guard stands.
These are things we know,
we observe,
that are embedded,
deep in our subconscious.

The pace is gentle.
Familiar faces pass.
The mind drifts,
but the body cross-checks
what is new,
and what is not.

It is quiet.
It is dark.
Just the glow
reflecting off
the wet tarmac,
and there is nowhere else
I would rather be.

2. The 42.2km Shoe

The shoe that runs with me.
an extension of my body,
the sole of my run.

I find the one,
and for that block of time,
I am committed.
A faith:
it will carry me so completely,
I forget they are on my feet.

Propulsion
when I am tired,
bounce
when I need the push,
grip
that holds me
to the ground.

Loop and loop again,
knot and knot again,
a quiet ritual.

It is the 42.2 km shoe.

The witness of my distance,
the keeper of my miles.

And when I finish the distance,
I retire it,
give it a place,
forever in the home.

It sits as my marker,
not of years,
but of the distance I have run,
and the roads
I have known.

3. Pockets

I love pockets.
Never enough pockets.
Gels and snacks,
emergency pods.
Phone and water,
electrolytes.
Car keys, taxi money.
More gels, more water.

And when the road stretches,
and the body says no,
you reach in,
grip the answer,
and go.

4. My Village

To run takes a village.

A village to hold you up
when you are tired and defeated.
To feed you and hydrate you.
To map out a city route,
to follow you through a race.
To squeeze you out of sweaty, sticky clothes
that bind your body.

The village takes care of your children,
your work, your home, when you run.
They let you sleep through family dinners,
movies and social outings.
They shout your name the loudest
as you stumble over a hill, gasping for breath.
They are your emergency contact,
bounding towards the medical tent.
They hold your hand
when you cry through pain of the body or mind.
They tell strangers, with pride,
that you ran a long run this morning.
They wear your medal,
strutting around the house,

knowing they are equal partners in the journey.

The village is kind
when you need kindness.
Tough
when you need to get back on the training block.
Funny
when laughter is what saves you.
They travel with you around the world,
pick up racing bibs,
locate routes and coffee shops.

To the village - I salute you.
To the leader of them all - my partner,
I run for *you* every day.

5. Raw Truth

Shush.
Noone wants to talk about it.
Something runners
must discover alone.
That is the way.

Burns, bruises, stings.
Redness,
like a scorching flame
has touched your skin.
All is revealed,
only as one removes the layers.
That last layer of skin is raw.

It is that scar of work done,
of runs delivered through heat,
rain and humidity.
It is the mark of friction,
the imprint of distance.
And all it takes to stop it all,
is that stick of cream.

But on those odd days
when those burns return,

and I yelp in pain
as water strikes my skin.
I am reminded of the work done,
and proud of the scar that remains.

6. Switch Off, Switch On

There is no sleep,
Like post run slumber.
The light switches off,
as my body slumps
into another world,
like circuits gone silent,
their power at rest.

A world where every atom,
every cell is recharging.
From being conscious
and eyes wide open,
to being switched off,
like a machine.
One switch, off.

There are two paths
that spark the switch again.
The first is with a jolt!
The recharge is not over,
but the world awake is filled with
little humans and a husband,
causing a sudden break in the matrix,
with their daily shenanigans.

The other when your eyes open gently,
a calm wave washes through,
as you reboot your brain
into the world that is awake.
Switch, on.

The only time one ever feels
this switch off and on,
is those first three months
when your child is born.
Filled with exhaustion the body
and spirit stays on,
like circuits still humming
till the power is gone.

The mind is a powerful machine.
Through stillness
it elevates your entire being,
And for that,
I am eternally grateful.
So now,
I switch off.

7. The Teacher

Lessons whisper softly,
but the road shouts them loud,
With every step, you learn-
Running is your teacher now.

Running teaches you *Courage*,
courage to face impossible distance,
to travel to unknown places,
to run deserted roads and trails.
It inspires us to be brave,
and fight the pain in our bodies,
and the defeat in our head.
It is this courage
that makes us grateful to face
our daily lives,
and stand tall,
with clear mind and heart,
we learn to survive.

Running keeps you *Honest*.
You cannot circumvent the process.
By telling untruths to yourself,
failure is inevitable.
You must be truthful,

to the body and to the mind,
and most of all,
to the rigour of the grind.
There are no short-cuts.
There is only the honest road.

Running is often a two-sided coin,
allowing you to experience life's emotions.
With Courage you must also face *Fear*,
fear of the pace
that reads too intense on paper,
fear of not being able to chase a time,
fear of not meeting your expectations,
or worse, those laid upon you.
From fear arises the strength,
to tread the path taken by
less than one percent.

Running makes you *Humble*.
It forces you to fail,
And try again.
Fall and get up,
body broken and bleeding,
gasping for air,
and find your breath again.

Running teaches you *Joy*,

The satisfaction of small milestones,
And gratitude for the big ones.
It reveals the power of simple things-
stormy skies, dusk and dawn,
urban oases and rural landscapes.
If the mind is clouded with life,
as you run,
a moment comes,
when you are struck by
a bolt of pure joy,
that clears the cloud
and fills the soul.

Running teaches us
to be *Alone*.
No one can run for you.
This is a journey you take alone,
in your mind,
and with your body .
The discipline to understand
the truth of being with yourself,
and accepting all of you,
with the faults and dents;
that is a powerful lesson learnt.

But most of all,
Running teaches you *Faith*;

To have faith in your legs,
your lungs,
your arms and your feet.
Faith in small increments;
to reach the next marker,
the next traffic light,
the next crater in the road,
the next curve and post.

Faith in the process,
which is long and arduous.
When the mind and body are pushed so far,
the world becomes blurred.
Legs keep moving
but the rest is failing.
The body may break down,
be injured or worse.
But with all we learn-
with courage and honesty,
fear and humility,
and once again,
run the road again.
At the moment
we have faith
that there is indeed,
in this world,
something larger than us.

Running is a continuous teacher of life,
it continues to empowers us
with a lessons of time.
Step forward, rise,
no time to relent-
this is the life of the less than one percent.

8. Mumbai Risers

The ones who rise before the sun,
When the city is sleeping,
We are the people
that draw our energy,
from the stillness of that time.

The sari clad lady striding up the fly over.
Her sneakers are in sight,
her sari hitched just above the ankles.
There is determination
in her every stride.
A focus like no other,
to get to the other side.

Then I see the head light.
I see them,
my heart is filled with delight!
He leads the way with his steady pace,
His cadence gentle and clear.
Step in step with him is the other,
with a light strapped on his forehead,
he is right behind.
They are bound by a tether
that connects their waists.

17

They have run for years,
one behind the other,
bound together in stride.
One with sight and the other with heart.
They truly are,
the purest testament,
of the love of the Run,
And the true power
of the ability to guide.

There are the legends who run powerfully
Through the rise and fall of the city roads.
Familiarity through the faces I see and
their gaits from afar,
revealing discipline and rigour
are their running code.

The old man with silver hair,
Lean and light-footed,
always starts with a walk.
By the time I loop round,
he has begun his run.
With a stride that has
the grace of tremendous experience,
he glides through the city streets,
clocking mile after mile,
while for many

the day has not yet begun.

The husband and wife and the dog.
Walking side by side,
and sometimes a meter apart.
You can sense the days
they don't see eye to eye,
But they never miss that walk before dawn.
Together they arrive,
and together they depart.

The young man with the beard,
who blasts off like a speed rocket
from the beaches of Chowpatty,
to the curved bench on Marine Drive.
The routine calls for reps,
From push ups to press-ups.
He exudes the discipline,
of the armed or naval forces,
an energy that spreads through the air,
and is powered from within.

Once the light
appears in the sky,
the runners emerge,
and from all directions,
the energy on the city roads

is amplified.
But it is before the light,
in the darkness of the morning,
where I find a familiarity, a comfort,
in the ones who rise.
The Mumbai Risers are my constant.
They are the moving markers,
through the silent streets
of the city that never sleeps,
and there is nowhere else,
I would rather be.

9. Bus-stop Drop

I run from my run
to drop
my children at the bus-stop.

This ritual is ingrained
in the rhythm of the morning.
I must get there on time,
rain or shine,
to gather bags and brace for
the last-minute tussle with the boys,
to walk and talk
about the day ahead,
while sweat drips
from head to toe.

My taxi-wallahs wait,
engines humming,
ferrying me from
Marine Drive's quiet waves,
to the beautiful chaos of my children's lives.
I have my regular wallahs,
driving slowly behind me,
anticipating the end of my run,
each with a signature style

and a familiar smile.

Bus-stop drop,
ritual, marker, finish line.
Run done, day begun,
chaos, laughter, motion,
non-stop,
heart still running,
smiling,
alive.

10. Run the Land

Step.
Breathe.
Move.

Paths curve,
hills rise,
forests whisper.

Feet press,
earth shifts,
stones, mud, roots.

Eyes open,
sky wide,
air alive.

Birds call,
insects hum,
leaves crackle.

Step.
Breathe.
Run.

The path narrows,
then opens.
Light shifts,
shade folds.

Land lifts, falls,
vistas spill,
horizon stretches.

Breath rises,
breath falls,
heart beats.

Curiosity pulls,
courage pushes,
bend after bend.

Peak comes,
sun bursts,
euphoria floods,
soul lifts.

Step.
Run.
Take the Risk

Move Forward
Run the land.

11. Ode to Toenails

You protect my toes,
and for that I am grateful.

Through the battering
of weather and shoes,
you have turned black and blue.

Some are clear, some dark, some lost.
Some covered with colors
to hide the damage.

Some pain to remind us of distance run,
some bruising too.

A part often missed,
Yet it bears the daily weight.
Toes hold our journeys.

To you,
I express my gratitude.

12. Study Notes

Being in my forties,
when I started to run,
meant making notes,
to execute the plan.

Thursday plans,
are especially daunting,
with progressive tempos,
intervals,
ramp downs,
and more.

What this means is,
I study the night before.
meticulously writing each
warm up,
stride,
activation,
cool down,
and then comes the ultimate outpour,
of every raw emotion –
fear,
anxiety,
and concern,

of being able to achieve,
all these paces through the straights and turns,

There is a blue and white,
trusted note book on my bedside,
where each of the plans,
are mapped out,
and written in my own lingo,
and shorthand,
to make sure I understand.
I then rip off the page,
and transport it to my bedside,
hoping that through the night,
I might imbibe,
through my sleeping spirit,
the crazy intensity of the ride.

All this is attributed to,
the man,
who has the wisdom,
and knowledge,
of the run,
my Coach.

Often at night,
post my studying delight,
I find myself messaging him,

the anxiety of the might
of the run he has planned.
In typical,
hard-core,
coaching style,
he replies,
using his words,
but the messaging is clear-
Get it done.

The irony then lay,
when I talked of this skill,
to my master of running,
He shared-
there is no need,
to get into the details,
that seems to
burden your mind.
To read and understand is key,
but beyond that-
Let it be.
Let your body and mind,
execute the plan,
naturally.

The surprise
the next day,

When the run was done.
I felt exhilarated,
for finishing what seemed impossible,
on the night of the study run.

But habits are hard to break,
when you run,
and nearing 48!
So my trusted white and blue book,
Remains by bedside,
To assure me on Thursdays,
That I can face
the might of the Run.

But often the secret lies,
in running from the heart,
which is the knowledge
that great coaches impart.

13. Running Armour

Shade, shield, and compass,
my cap guards from sun and rain
the run begins here.

Moulded to my form,
salt and time have shaped its brim,
stories in the weave.

My city stitched bold,
wind hums its name as I move,
we run, side by side.

14. The Route

A slight rise
at the gate of my building,
from there that I begin.
With the rise and fall
of the asphalt,
the flyover comes ahead,
bringing a great sense of comfort,
and no sense of dread.

Then a straight shot
past large stone walls,
sleeping watchmen,
and the petrol station.
A sharp turn to the right,
and it is best to stay on the pavement,
as the corner is blind,
and often cars comes racing,
with no conscience in mind.

The bells of the temple
can be heard as I draw closer.
The cacophony of the neighbourhood,
is loud and clear.

From a distance
I see the sharp left,
and onto the straight
that runs parallel,
to the beach and the sea.

The sidewalk is filled
with bus-stops,
and entries to gardens,
and gymkhanas,
where people meet and greet.

From the road to the promenade,
a switch in the surface,
from asphalt to paver stones,
and then concrete.

A flyover rises above from the ground,
while a tunnel begins,
on the other side,
way down.

Some markers are clear,
like large traffic lights
with signs to drive slow,
and less monumental ones,
like railings and trees,

and small bumps in the roads.

The straight along the water,
is silent and calming,
The humidity and wind is high,
and often alarming.

Keep going straight
to the south of the island,
past government and railways,
and slum-dwellers houses.
through the small streets
of old South Mumbai.
The landmark of a church
at the edge
of the cantonment is reached.
Loop round and back,
towards the old cinemas,
port walls,
historic buildings,
all stand majestic and tall,
as markers of time.

Through small *gulleys* I run,
passing by children
dressed in jerseys,
emblazoned with Messi and Ronaldo,

their laughter and chatter,
in match with my tempo.

The buildings of justice,
and education rise high,
surrounding the lush green maidens,
where cricketers and walkers alike,
inhale the open space of the city,
Pass the big clock tower,
who sets the time for us all,
and garbage trucks lined up,
clearing the city's haul.

Art Deco buildings,
one after the other,
with cars parked in front,
so there is no clear path ahead,
but I weave through,
making sure I balance,
the width of the space.

Then back,
to the open edge of the sea,
where I am greeted,
by the dogs and the cats that retreat,
into corners
of benches and shops,

to find refuge from people
and the weather that is hot.

The route always changes
from time to time.
So much to explore,
and so many layers to find.
Each one with its people,
its architecture,
its sounds,
carving out images
to entertain the mind.

There is no place in the world,
I would rather be
than Mumbai.
Near the sand and the sea.
She is the heart of my run,
and will always remain,
There is always,
a new story,
a new spirit,
in every route that I take.

15. Symphony in Motion

As a classical dancer,
I learnt young,
the power of synergy,
music and body moving as one.
That rhythm found its way
into the ethos of my runs.

Music has stayed
through trials and tribulations,
dull days and restless nights,
moments of peace,
and flashes of salvation.
It carries every human emotion,
settling deep within,
a song that hums
decades on.

Running is the same,
a rising spirit through life.
Both are symbiotic,
guides through chaos and calm,
darkness and light.

From Indian *raagas*

to classic rock,
electronic beats
to pop anthems,
the soundtrack shifts
with the road beneath.
You choose your BPM,
the rhythm that matches your breath,
propelling you on
to the next marker,
the next race,
the next revelation.

Each run has its score,
an opener that lifts,
a mid-beat that steadies,
a crescendo that drives you
beyond what you thought you could.
It flows through urban and rural,
seamless with scene and mood,
raising the soul,
fueling the body.

Sometimes it fades,
a hum, white noise,
blending with breath and stride,
carrying you forward
into quiet transcendence.

Music creates a world
of joy, hope, release,
the very reasons
you run with ease.

So fault me not
for the music I choose,
each runner crafts her own rhythm,
her own space
of beat, voice, and bass.

Let it transport you
as your feet find flight,
one step, one song,
re-energised,
re-engaged,
alive in the run.

16. The Runner's Hump

We carry a hump,
a sloshy blob,
our badge of pride
and awkward job.

A pack of water
on our back,
that burps and gurgles
down the track.

Hydration tech,
so sleek, so bold,
basically Tupperware
for liquid gold.

It hugs too tight,
it rubs, it squeaks,
it makes us sound
like walking leaks.

The pipe dangles near
a teasing straw,
you sip mid-stride,
and spill on your jaw.

Yet come kilometre thirty,
you whisper its name,
this sweaty hump
has saved your game.

So here's to the pack,
the bounce, the bump,
the slosh, the splash,
the runner's hump.

It's love. It's hate.
It bumps, it drains.
We curse its weight,
we praise its gains,
and still, it runs with us again.

17. The Discipline of No

No to late nights,
to parties that stretch till dawn.
No to the easy laughter of friends,
lingering over beers
on the gymkhana lawns.

No to movies,
to dinners that run too long.
No to the joy of spontaneity,
the music, the dance, the song.

No to junk food,
no to indulgent plates.
No to careless mornings,
no to sleeping late.

No to birthdays missed,
to celebrations set aside.
No to being fully present,
when the long run waits outside.

No to comfort,
to warmth beneath the sheets.
No to idle wandering,

to slow unhurried streets.

No to excuses,
to weakness, to doubt.
No to the tempting voice
that whispers, "Sit this one out."

Training demands subtraction,
a pruning of life's excess,
each "no" becomes
a sharper "yes."

Yes to focus.
Yes to purpose.
Yes to discipline,
and all it shapes within.

The marathon takes,
but it also gives,
a rare clarity of what it means
to choose,
to commit,
to live.

18. This Husband of Mine

This husband of mine,
my partner in crime,
who trails me in Birkenstocks,
on the other side of the line.

While I am running,
and racing,
he stares at his phone,
plots my next stop,
to catch me in stride
at the next spot.

Black coffee in hand,
every few miles,
he leaps on subways,
hustles through streets,
just to keep me in sight.

He is always present,
in my heart, in my mind,
as I push through the corners
with pain in my side.

He comes charging with force

to the medical tent,
raving and ranting
that this race must end.

But minutes later
he's back on my trail,
fast-walking behind me,
until his sandals fail.

Chasing the run,
we travel through India
and across the world.
His one condition,
holds simple and true:
the run is my passion,
the food is his due.
A race and a feast,
a journey for two.

He is my North Star,
the end of the line.
Every day I am grateful
that he is all mine.

19. Women Who Run

A night run with women.
Force. Unleashed.
Through the streets.
Of the city I love.
That awakens the beast.

We shed the layers-
mother, sister,
daughter, wife,
worker, maker.

We rise as one.
Pure in form.
Resilience blazing.
Strength reborn.

We are grit.
We are fire.
Alpha women.
Rising higher.

We are strong.
We are brave.
Warriors of the night.

Energy released.
Together as one.

This is the true power.
Women who run.

20. Timekeeper

Velcro on my hand,
you govern the time
distance and pace,
laps, heart-rate.

You glow in the dark
when I lift my wrist,
truth on display:
how much more to persist.

Swiping through faces,
stride after stride,
peering at quadrants,
numbers compiled
where the truth resides.

Your beeps are a signal,
a rhythm, a call.
We dread the first,
we crave the last,
counting down
every fall.

Emblazoned in silver,

the words of a legend:
A Running World is a Better World.
Signed- Eliud Kipchoge.
May his fire propel me,
his spirit inspire,
keeping me honest,
keeping me true.

Yet there are runs
when I don't look down,
the body keeps time,
the rhythm within.
Those moments are freedom,
untethered, unbound,
released from the numbers,
released from the ground.

Still, you remain
a sacred possession.
One finger waiting
on the red button.
Press-
the gunshot rings,
legs surge forward.
Press again-
and all is still.

To the watch on my wrist:
guide me,
push me,
teach me persistence.
Carry me always
to the end of the line,
until I press the red button
that stops the time.

21. To My Boys

Will my children love running
the way I do?
The routine, the rigour,
the joys and the aches,
the stubborn glutes,
the weary knees?

Will they run through rain,
breathe in fresh earth,
trace city streets
to discover new routes?

Will they cherish the zone,
that quiet space,
and the worth it builds
deep within?

Will they learn the lessons
the distance reveals,
the pain, the glory,
the courage to heal?

Will they be curious,
brave,

ready to run on their own
through a world that is tough,
a battle zone?

I hope they will find
what I have found,
a passion to love,
a fire to hold.

Will my boys inherit
the road I knew?
Deep inside my heart,
I secretly hope they do.